SUCCESS STRATEGIES
of
IMMIGRANT LEADERS
IN THE UNITED STATES

Why Some Individuals Succeed
While Others Don't

Dr. Shelly M. Cameron

Copyright © 2017

by

Shelly M. Cameron, EdD

Success Strategies of Immigrant Leaders in the United States

All rights reserved. No part of this publication may be reproduced, distributed, or transmitted in any form or by any means, including photocopying, recording, or other electronic or mechanical methods, without the prior written permission of the author or publisher, except in the case of brief quotations embodied in critical reviews and certain other noncommercial uses permitted by copyright law.

ISBN: 978-0-692-86596-5 (Authors in Press

ISBN-10: 0692865969

Library of Congress in-Publication Data

Dr. Cameron, Shelly

www.shellycameron.com

First Printing 2017

Printed in United States of America

Contributors

Dale Holness, Pauline Grant, Dr. Charlene Desir, Mariela Cardona, Dr. Susan Davis, Clinton Weekes, Phillip Goombs, Linda Odum, Winston Barnes, Dr. Winston Alexis, Dr. Tatiana Martinez

Dedicated to my two girls

Monique & Ashleigh

"With Every Success Comes Celebration"

Elaine Cameron-Walters

CONTENTS

ACKNOWLEDGEMENTS ix
PREFACE...xi
   How to Read This Book xiii

SECTION 1: SUCCESS: THE MINDSET 1
CHAPTER 1: SUCCESS..3
   It Starts With a Dream 4
   Dreamers 5
   Success Redefined 7
   Entrepreneurs and Success 9
   Caution: Success and Stress 11
CHAPTER 2: DO YOU HAVE WHAT IT TAKES?....13
   Trait Approach 14
   Overcoming Failure – Learning...17
CHAPTER 3: TOP 15 LEADERSHIP TRAITS 21
   Top 15 Leadership Traits...21

SECTION 2: THE STUDY 25
CHAPTER 4: CARIBBEAN AMERICANS
IMMIGRANTS: WHO ARE THEY? 27
   Evolution in the United States 28
   Caribbean American Heritage Month..............................31
   Study Participants...33

CHAPTER 5: THE UNVEILING: NARRATIVES OF THEIR JOURNEY 35

CHAPTER 6: CHALLENGES ALONG THE WAY 49

CHAPTER 7: NEW CULTURE: STEPS TO SUCCESS 55

CHAPTER 8: THE COMPARISON WITH OTHER ETHNIC GROUPS 61

   Iranian Americans Versus Caribbean Americans 62

CHAPTER 9: NOW IT'S YOUR TURN 65

EPILOGUE 71

DEFINITION OF TERMS 73

REFERENCES 77

ABOUT THE AUTHOR 89

ACKNOWLEDGEMENTS

As I reflect on the journey that immigrants have trod and especially the narratives of the leaders whose stories were explored in this book, it caused me to reflect on the path that I have traveled on this quest to complete this book and leave something tangible behind. Amidst my own personal reflection on this journey I want to express my heartfelt gratitude to my mother, Hermie Daley-Muir who planted the seed on the very day of my master's degree graduation. Although she and my younger sibling Carleen did not live to see me cross the finish line, they were there to ignite the fire, and for that I am forever grateful. I would also like to say an abundance of thanks to my two daughters, Monique and Ashleigh, whose tolerance and support are beyond words. This was all for you.

Most important, I would like to say thanks to Dr. Karen Bowser, for her wisdom, patience and encouragement, and for listening to my thoughts and ideas for youths and helping me to carve it into something concrete and useful. Thanks also to my editor, Dr. Lorraine Maslow, for her time and expertise in editing this book. In addition, my sincere gratitude to Dr. Fereshteh Amin, who felt the same haunting urge to write on behalf of Iranian Americans whose work I replicated and cemented to the Caribbean American populace.

Above all, thanks to my mentor and friend Duke, for his encouragement and for providing me with the impetus that forced me to achieve my best potential. Thanks to my uncle, Dr. Adolph Cameron, the forerunner in whose path I have closely followed. Thanks to my sister Maxine, my father Lionel, my aunt Kathleen, and the rest of the family who believed in me and were my greatest cheerleaders. Last, special thanks to my friends who not only encouraged but prayed that with God all things are possible.

Finally, special thanks to my study participants, the Immigrant leaders who willingly participated in this research, shared their stories and made it possible. I am grateful for the opportunity to add to literature on Immigrants with the hope that it will stimulate the potential for success amongst youths, other ethnic groups, and future generations.

PREFACE

He was the second of four children. A great table tennis player who played for the little island of Jamaica. He represented the country, but it wasn't enough to keep him occupied. Sadly, one day his privileges were pulled. He hung around for a while. Eventually, he got a job working as merchandiser with a healthcare company. After working there for several years, he lost his job. He suddenly felt despondent, as if there was no reason to live.

Between the ages of 30-35, he tried several odd jobs, not getting anything he really wanted. He looked at his family members—they were successful professionals, but what was happening to him? He had gone to a good high school, graduated, yet wasn't able to hold down a job, to make a living. He had one child, a son. What was the example he was setting for his son; he questioned himself?

So he followed his passion for cars and driving. He decided to become a taxi driver; driving people up and down, back and forth to their various destinations. As luck would have it, he even lost that job because he did not earn enough to maintain the car.

Despondent, he turned to marijuana. The "weed" always made things seem a little better. When things got tough, he smoked more weed to "make things better." In his 30s, a call came to his family that he had been stabbed several times and shot—later described as a mistake. A misunderstanding. But he was dead. Dead at a young age, leaving his son with no father to care for him.

This is the story of one youth. One man who succumbed to a life of apathy. A life embroiled with a lackadaisical spirit from dusk till dawn. A life that succumbed to a spirit of meaninglessness.

Sadly, this is not an isolated case. It is common among youths from many backgrounds. It is common to youths throughout the United States. Research reveals that there are more Black youths in prisons in the United States compared to other ethnicities. I reflected on what could be done to positively influence youths who are sitting by idly. Visit inner city communities and one will find many just 'chilling'—awaiting life to happen.

Therefore, I decided to conduct research through collaborating with Nova Southeastern University and individuals who are successful Caribbean Americans in the United States—immigrant leaders who have achieved success in business, media, healthcare, education, government, aviation, politics, and more. What could those youths who were hanging around, loitering on plazas, learn from those who have made it, who were born under similar circumstances just like them, yet became successful? What is the difference? Is there a difference? And can these differences be taught to counter the problem?

The goal of this book is to provide youths and ethnic minorities with the strategies of how to be successful.

Readers will be exposed to the traits of successful Caribbean Americans, the challenges they encountered after migration, strategies they used to overcome the challenges, and the factors that most influenced their success. Finally, a comparative analysis is included to ascertain whether the challenges are common to other ethnic groups with similar issues.

Join us as we embark on this journey to those areas that youths and individuals in transition can take to become successful in their lives.

How to Read This Book

This book is divided into two parts. The first provides the framework for the book and the second speaks directly to the study. Read the preface which provides the context and rationale for writing this book. Chapter one provides some background on the setting. It gives information on the terms that formed the basis of this book. Terms such as the American dream, dreamers, leaders, leadership and success are explored. Chapter two is one of my absolute favorites since it provides stories of the failures and subsequent success of some of society's well known leaders. How they failed and what propelled them to move on towards their goals. Chapter three reveals the 15 leadership traits unveiled in the research. The meanings of the different traits are explained. You will find it intriguing if you look closely to identify any of your own personal traits.

We step into the second part of the book which shares details of the study with the immigrant Leaders who participated in the interviews. For immigrants who have never given a single thought to this topic, Chapter four provides historical information on waves of immigration and the different paths Caribbean Nationals have trod from the United Kingdom then into the United States. The chapter ends describing the study participants. Names have been changed to protect their identity.

Chapters five through seven exposes the narratives of the leaders as they explain the stories of their journey, the challenges they experienced along the way as well as the strategies they used to overcome the challenges. I implore you to look closely at the narratives to see if you can identify with any experience you encountered.

As we draw closer to the finale, chapter eight shares that this study was replicated from a similar study done on Iranian Americans. A comparison between Iranian Americans and Caribbean Americans was discussed to assess whether both groups of immigrants shared similar experiences or if they differed, to what extent.

The book concludes giving ideas on how you as an ethnic minority, youth or new immigrant can achieve your goals in your new country. Surprising revelations are unveiled in the Epilogue. In a nutshell, read the chapters in any manner you wish. The book can be kept as a reference for those who want to be kept motivated and inspired to overcome challenges in their new country. In essence it provides the rationale why some people succeed while others don't. Cheers to your Success!

SECTION 1
SUCCESS: THE MINDSET

CHAPTER 1

SUCCESS

The starting point of all achievement is desire.
-Napoleon Hill

Maria Rodriquez arrived in the United States with her family when she was 12 years old. Her parents left her at home to care for her little brother while they went off in pursuit of the American dream. She was from Cuba, the largest island in the Caribbean, where her parents left all they had to escape the Castro regime. Countless days and nights were spent fighting for a better life. Maria was fair, so her ethnicity was always mistaken as White. But her inability to speak the language left many confused. After graduating from high school, she went to college then dropped out because she got married. But pregnancy changed her life. She promised her unborn son that she would make sure he had the best life. That promise resulted in her reenrollment in college, where she decided to study journalism. She later captured one of the top spots in the field. Maria now manages one of South Florida's top media stations.

So, what does success look like? How does it feel? Does it follow the pattern of the movie *The Pursuit of Happyness*? More specifically, what does it take to be successful? Can anyone achieve success? Is it limited to only the rich and famous? These questions have been asked by many individuals who have a desire to become successful—to achieve the American Dream.

Success is not always linear. To be clear, let's define success. The term *success* refers to the attainment of wealth, position, and honors. More importantly, success means different things to different people. Essentially, it means getting what a person wants with rewards that are sustainable for individuals and those for whom they care. Fereshteh Amin shared components of her research about high achievers: happiness, achievement, significance, and legacy. Success that encompasses all four kinds of accomplishments is more enriching and lasting. So how can we achieve this success?

It Starts With a Dream

For most, the American Dream is all about the idea of achieving success. This not only involves a high income and a secure job, but it is the notion that even those who are poor and have limited skills can succeed. Various facets emphasize a life that embraces freedom and self-fulfillment, opportunities fuel the realization of the dream. Without opportunities, the dream remains just that—a dream. There are many whose dreams have become real, and that has encouraged immigration. To many, the dream provides the chance to make money.

The process of attaining the American Dream is the process of becoming middle class, which in essence means moving up the socioeconomic status ladder, becoming homeowners in communities, and participating in the political process. As Clarke and Henke asserted, the concomitants of the middle class include material goods; homeownership with at least one car; consumer items such as televisions, dishwashers, technological gadgets; the funds to educate and raise healthy children; and the ability to provide support for a comfortable retirement.

Dreamers

Autobiographical stories were written by students and Educators for Fair Consideration. This is a San Francisco-based nonprofit organization that provides direct support and advocacy for low-income immigrant students who have grown up in the United States but face challenges because of financial need and immigration status. These students shed light on what it is like to grow up as undocumented youths. They talked about not being able to return to their homelands, wanting to be accepted as Americans, and the fear of living in the shadows (Hernandez, Mendez, Lio, Latthi, & Eusebio).

One student reflected on the morning of the destruction of the World Trade Center's Twin Towers. He remembered the pain seen on his teacher's face. He lamented that he, too, wanted to feel the same pain. He wanted to experience the same closeness to the nation. He wanted to become a part of the infinite American family, that when one part hurts, he would hurt also.

Another student reflected on past memories. His memories were of the debt collection problems his parents faced in Thailand. He reflected on their subsequent escape to Milpitas, California. There, his parents, brother, and sister crammed into a one-bedroom apartment. He reflected on his mother's postsurgical pain when he had to call her gynecologist to explain her pains months after her surgery because there was no Thai translator. He vowed then that he would become a doctor.

Four ways noncitizens may pursue either temporary or permanent residency in the United States in their attempt to build a better life and achieve the American Dream. These are (a) apply on humanitarian grounds (such as asylum seekers who face persecution in their home country); (b) have a United States citizen family member petition (but applications may take up to 10 to 20 years to become eligible if they do not have a family member); (c) have an employer sponsor (but quotas are low for the unskilled and it is an expensive process that most employers are unwilling to pursue); and (d) marry a United States citizen (but relationship status is not enough to obtain residency). These ways are the only hope noncitizens have to achieve the American Dream (Filisko, 2012).

Success Redefined

Many have asked for success to be redefined. Why? Because of the rationale that personal success in the business environment holds no guarantees and rapid shifts in demands and opportunities require individuals to pay attention to a number of key factors. This is necessary because the traditional dream of rising from the mailroom to the boardroom based on talent and loyalty no longer exists. Many factors contribute to success. In the study of outliers, Malcolm Gladwell contended that the true story of success is very different, and if individuals want to understand how some people thrive, they should spend more time looking around them at such things as their family, their birthplace, or even their birth date. Successful people do not do it alone. They are products of particular places and environments. Success arises out of the steady accumulation of advantages: when and where an individual was born, what their parents did for a living, and the circumstances of their upbringing. Success is a function of persistence and doggedness and the willingness to work hard. Success is not exceptional or mysterious. It is grounded in a web of advantages and inheritances. Some advantages are deserved, and some are not; some are earned, and some are based on luck;

but all are critical attributes to making them who they are.

As we advance into the 21st century, individuals should ensure that they possess skills that are already inherent, but individuals tend to underutilize their abilities. Hall-of-Famer Berg suggested five strategies to personal success that may prove useful. These are simply aim, anticipation, audacity, action, and adaptability.

Through *aim,* individuals should create a personal definition of success. Ask yourself what your goals are and what success looks like to you. To achieve goals, individuals *anticipate* through creating everything twice, first in their minds and then in physical reality. Through *audacity*, individuals should get rid of negative attitudes and fear of failure or disapproval, which is a critical barrier to success and should be avoided at all cost. A focus on *action* helps individuals overcome destructive habits such as indecisiveness, procrastination, and overplanning. Individuals should act as though they have already succeeded through affiliating with successful people; maintaining learning, mental, and physical fitness; and rewarding small successes. Finally, flexibility is important in the application of *adaptability*. Lack of adaptability leads to overcommitment to activities at which people are sure they can succeed rather than risking the pain of possible failure in pursuit of new achievements.

Entrepreneurs and Success

Success is in the attempt rather than the outcome. "It is in at least trying," said one entrepreneur. Buchholz, in his book *New Ideas from Dead CEOs,* spoke about truly successful people who had passed on. Most of these people achieved society's accolades and became household names, including Estee Lauder, Mary Kay, and Ray Kroc who established McDonald's. Common qualities among these entrepreneurs were persistence in the face of more than a few obstacles (at times hundreds and even thousands) and a spirit of innovation in an era when the Internet and rapid technology were nowhere to be found. They had to think outside the box to get their ideas into the hands of consumers, business leaders, and the affluent in society, both locally and globally. They had the dedication and determination to succeed no matter what the odds. Most important, they had a plan and a strategy to succeed, a never-give-up attitude. For example, Estee Lauder, in her quest to reach affluent consumers in prestigious department stores, once spilled an expensive bottle of perfume on purpose. The sweet-smelling fragrance of the perfume permeated the store. Shoppers liked the scent, and the rest is history.

The secrets of success of entrepreneurs were revealed at the Business Hall of Fame in Washington, DC. Recipients believed that the secret to their success included mentoring, perseverance, unified vision and passion, being prepared, taking risks, getting along with people, doing the right thing, and not being satisfied.

John Wooden's memoir titled *Lessons From a Legend* revealed Wooden's success as a person and as a coach. Lessons included (a) the stance that sports do not build character but reveal it, (b) individuals must pay attention to details, (c) individuals should be careful of complacency by being quick but not hurrying, (d) individuals should also act with integrity, and (e) individuals should build a foundation for success. Wooden's Pyramid of Success indicated that at the top of the pyramid was *competitive greatness*. On the levels leading up to it were key milestones such as *loyalty, friendship*, and *team spirit*. Winning or losing is a byproduct of individual preparation (Forck).

The factors contributing to the success of entrepreneurs in developing countries was studied. Factors found to be significant in determining success were the level of family support, good customer service, charisma, friendliness to customers, business stress, ability to manage personnel, previous business experience, hard work, appropriate training, satisfactory government support, political involvement, and being married (Kara, Chu, & Benzing).

Caution: Success and Stress

To place a twist on attaining success, one wonders whether the good life is always good. Are the very things that so many individuals strive for, such as a high-paying and powerful job, a beautiful house, a wardrobe of nice clothes in desirable sizes, and a fancy education for children to prepare them for carrying on this way of life: Do these very things turn out to be more trouble than they are worth? In fact, it is believed that the psychological burdens associated with being a low-status individual (i.e., poor) grow lighter as people move up the social ladder, but that is true only to a certain extent. Once individuals achieve more success, the mental and physical health benefits associated with greater affluence fade away. As individuals near the top, life stress increases dramatically, and its toxic effects essentially cancel out many positive aspects of succeeding.

The stress of high status is also a reason for caution. Schieman, Yuko, and Van Gundy found that people with higher levels of education and in higher status occupations with higher income experience higher levels of stress. Some factors that contribute to stress include more authority and autonomy, nonroutine work demands, involvement, and longer hours, may lead to more conflicts between work and home. This was attributed to the rationale that the very trappings of success can make life harder for those who are more driven and work devoted.

Power is another benefit that was identified as a stressor. Having authority over others binds people to all sorts of interpersonal conflicts and management turmoil, leading to very high stress. Likewise, the smaller details associated with micro-impression-management activities, such as getting the right clothes, the right haircut, and the big enough house, as well as raising the attractive, athletic, community-serving kids that will get into Harvard, all contribute to stress.

Furthermore, in high-status communities, such activities might be a requirement rather than a choice in order to maintain credibility. Individuals have to wear the right suit to work or have to live in the right neighborhood, or else people will not take them seriously. Because millions of Americans struggle to make ends meet and would probably be willing to trade places, *Time* magazine writer Warner warned, "Be careful what you wish for."

CHAPTER 2

DO YOU HAVE WHAT IT TAKES?

Success is not final: failure is not fatal: it is the courage to continue that counts.
-Winston Churchill

We often wonder if success comes only to individuals with certain traits or characteristics. Does it come to those who are able to lead themselves and others? Studies show this is a strong possibility. In the book *Moments,* author Charmaine Gooden-Monteith shared the thought that good things come to those who go after them, not to those who wait. This was evident in a conversation I had at a conference with a talented middle-aged gentleman who had risen to the pinnacle of success in the performing arts. When I asked about his next step for his career transition (which he was concerned about), he shared that he is waiting on opportunities. Puzzled, I sought clarification. He explained that his work speaks for itself. I found it necessary to advise him that those days are long gone.

No longer can individuals sit and wait on companies to call them for opportunities that they may be qualified for. In addition, with this age of rapid change in technologies, what made individuals like this gentleman successful before is no guarantee that it will happen again. Armed with internal traits, individuals must seek the opportunities, and more than likely they will be successful.

Following are highlights of the essentials of leadership, and the traits that can be seen.

Trait Approach

Leadership is considered a trait. Each individual brings certain inherent qualities that influence the way he or she leads. Some leaders are confident, some are decisive, and others are outgoing and sociable. Renowned leadership theorist Northouse, often stressed that leadership as a trait follows the argument that leaders are born and not made. Leadership is complex and includes many dimensions. For some people, leadership is a trait or ability; whereas for others, it is a skill or behavior; and for some, leadership is a relationship.

Leadership is an ability. A person who has the capacity to lead is considered a leader. Leadership is also a skill that is conceptualized as a competency developed to accomplish a task effectively. Skilled leaders are competent people who know the means and methods for carrying out their responsibilities.

Leadership is also a behavior that is observable. When someone leads, that individual's leadership behavior becomes visible which means that we can see it clearly.

Leadership is a relationship that is centered on the communication and collaboration between leaders and followers rather than on the unique qualities of the leader. This means working with and through people. A leader affects and is affected by followers. Both leaders and followers are affected in turn by the situation that surrounds them.

Positive Traits. Positive leadership qualities include being trustworthy and just, having foresight, confident, intelligent, win-win problem solver, administratively skilled, excellence oriented, decisive, motivational, communicative, coordinator, honest, encouraging, dependable, team builder, and informed. Effective leaders exhibit traits of intelligence, confidence, determination, integrity, and sociability (Northouse 2007).

Some attributes are essential for success. These include influence, because leadership is the ability to attract followers. Leaders' moral values are important because the leader's values must coincide with the values of followers; leadership is a process that never stops. Another key attribute of leadership is commitment, because committed leaders are neither bystanders nor people with a title or position. Followers must believe that leaders are in it for the long haul because the followers are relying on the leader for their future. Committed leaders seek challenging opportunities in which companies and employees can change, improve, and grow. Leadership also requires that some qualified risks must be taken and that leaders learn from past mistakes. A leader requires vision and the ability to engage people into that vision. In essence, a committed leader gets the people moving and then stands behind them with support (Greer, 2011).

Another key attribute of leadership is the ability to listen. This is important even when the leader has to hear things that he or she does not want to hear. The leader must hear the message even though history, anger, frustration, or hostility acts as a filter. Therefore, it is important to interpret the message to ensure mutual understanding. The leader should then evaluate the message through asking questions and analyzing the evidence to avoid jumping to conclusions. Finally, it is important for the leader to respond to the message through verbal or nonverbal feedback to ensure that the message was properly received.

Negative Traits. Negative leader traits include being a loner, irritable, ruthless, asocial, nonexplicit, dictatorial, uncooperative, and egocentric. The infamous Adolf Hitler is often referred to as the epitome of negative leadership. He has been described as determined to command personally. His behavior intrigued many and fell under what Northouse described as the psychodynamic theory of leadership behavior.

Undoubtedly, we recognize that leadership is complex and includes many dimensions. For some, leadership is a trait or ability. For others it is a skill or behavior and for others, leadership is a relationship.

Overcoming Failure – Learning

Remember, leadership and success are not always linear. Thomas Edison developed thousands of prototypes of the light bulb before he found the one that worked. Albert Einstein was unemployed for two years after he graduated college. Like Edison and Einstein, modern-day luminaries like Mark Cuban and J. K. Rowling, as Aaron Taube shared, were able to use their setbacks to push them forward. Several examples follow of extremely successful leaders who learned from their failures.

The late **Nelson Mandela**, a renowned leader, came under harsh criticism for his attempt to prevent the onset of civil war in South Africa. Delving deeper into Mandela's case, criticisms initially came from Black individuals claiming that Mandela made greater efforts when addressing issues for Whites than when addressing issues of Blacks. Despite that, Mandela ignored criticisms and addressed issues of Whites first, which consequently resulted in South Africa winning the rugby match that created unity in that nation (Eubanks et al., 2010).

Steve Jobs had a natural ability to lead. He started his business in his parents' garage. The company developed and grew. It attracted a board of directors that, in the end, fired him. Devastated but not to be deterred from his dream, Jobs started another company that focused mainly on software. Today, the world enjoys his innovations including Apple Watch, iPhone, iPad, iMac, and more.

Oprah Winfrey learned that failure is only an illusion after her cable network started off poorly. She said the worst time in her professional life came when the Oprah Winfrey Network's (OWN) ratings plummeted a year after launch. Later, in a Harvard commencement speech, Winfrey said that she told herself repeatedly that failure is an illusion. She said, "There is no such thing as failure. Failure is just life trying to move us in another direction. When you're down in the hole, when that moment comes, it's really okay to feel bad for a little while. Give yourself time to mourn what you think you may have lost—but then here's the key; learn from every mistake because every experience, encounter, and particularly your mistakes are there to teach you and force you into being more of who you are. Winfrey was able to get OWN moving in the right direction, and the network gained a profit in 2013 (Taube, 2014).

Dallas Mavericks owner **Mark Cuban**, prior to starting his first company, worked as a bartender, a short-order cook, and a carpenter. Cuban later told CNN that on multiple occasions, he would come home with a date only to find that the electricity had been turned off by the utility company. Cuban decided to have a positive outlook about his failures and made sure to learn something from his mistakes. He told Smart Business, "I've learned that it doesn't matter how many times you failed, you only have to be right once. I was an idiot lots of times, and I learned from them all."

Jay Z learned that his success needed to come from within after his second album flat-lined. Jay Z's first album, Reasonable Doubt, is considered by many to be one of the best rap albums of all time. His second album, In My Lifetime, wound up not being as successful commercially as his first, and he was not happy. He said, "I tried to make these records that were bigger and would be more popular, which was a failure. Going for that success really messed up that project and set a bad tone. It was a huge learning lesson for me that if I was going to be successful, I had to be successful with myself. I couldn't be successful doing what other people were doing. I had to do what I believed in and what felt real to me and true to me."

Failure gave **J.K. Rowling** the freedom to pursue her art. In 1993, the Harry Potter author was an unemployed single mother who saw herself as a failure. She later said, in a commencement speech at Harvard, that the experience actually helped her by getting rid of her fear of failure—which allowed her to focus on writing the stories that would ultimately become the Harry Potter novels. "Failure meant a stripping away of the inessential. I stopped pretending to myself that I was anything other than what I was and began to direct all my energy into finishing the only work that mattered to me. Had I really succeeded at anything else, I might never have found the determination to succeed in the one arena I believed I truly belonged. I was set free because my greatest fear had been realized, and I was still alive and I still had a daughter whom I adored, and I had an old typewriter and a big idea" (Taube, 2014).

So we gather from these examples of success that if you want to be successful, you must follow your heart, your passion. If you strongly believe something in your ability; Go for it! Reach for the stars! More than likely you will achieve with dedication and hard work. To lead yourself, you must believe in your ability.

CHAPTER 3

TOP 15 LEADERSHIP TRAITS

In order to succeed, we must first believe that we can.
                                            - Nikos Kazantzakis

Top 15 Leadership Traits

Research conducted among Caribbean American leaders found that the traits they believed contributed to their success were self-confidence, self-discovery, values, vision, humility, commitment, persistence, optimism, family oriented, creativity, drive, learner, communication skills, passion, and responsibility. Qualities of each trait is described.

Persistence refers to the desire to never give up in spite of all the odds.

Self-Confidence includes a sense of self-esteem and self-assurance and the belief that one can make a difference. It allows the leader to feel assured that his or her attempts to influence are appropriate and right.

Self-discovery pertains to an individual knowing his or her strengths, talents, and interests and what he or she can do well.

Values/ethics includes having true honesty and trustworthiness it provides a basis for understanding what it means to be a morally decent human being.

Vision is identified by the ability to envision an uplifting and ennobling future, to have a dream or mission, to see the pattern, and to establish goals for oneself. Its growth is exemplified through studying, reading, comparing, traveling, seeing, imagining, seeking, and analyzing activities to create and receive views of what is possible.

Humility typifies believing in good luck and possibilities beyond one's control, appreciating what life is giving, modest and willful, humble and fearless.

Commitment is related to establishing challenges and expectations and applying oneself with focus and patience. The more difficult a goal, the more commitment is essential.

Persistence. Following through, endurance, and not giving up in pursuit of goals are attributes of persistence. Others include exhibiting determination, initiative, and willingness to assert oneself, being proactive and having the ability to persevere in the face of obstacles.

Optimistic. An optimistic leader sees challenges as the beginning to a new success and willingness to tolerate frustration and delay with an optimistic outlook. An optimistic leader also has drive to achieve, seeing an opportunity even in the face of setbacks or failure.

Family oriented. This theme is characterized by respecting family values and familial influence including mother, father, and extended family.

Creativity. The components included in this theme are venturesome and originality in problem solving, thinking out of the box, and a multicultural problem-solving approach.

Drive. This is desire to do more and more and the determination to exercise initiative in social situations.

Learner refers to the desire for lifelong learning and a consistent pursuit for knowledge.

Communication skills. The qualities included in this theme are being articulate, having people skills and listening skills, speaking publicly, and being able to communicate ideas Being verbally involved, being informed, being firm but not rigid, seeking others' opinions, and initiating new ideas are also included.

Passion. This theme is defined by being passionate about what one is doing and putting one's heart into it, as well as connecting with the possibilities of the future and having the chance to do something about it.

Responsibility. This theme is identified by taking the responsibility for achieving what one believes is important and the willingness to accept the consequences of decisions and actions.

SECTION 2

THE STUDY

CHAPTER 4

CARIBBEAN AMERICANS IMMIGRANTS: WHO ARE THEY?

Always be yourself, express yourself, have faith in yourself, do not go out and look for a successful personality and duplicate it.

-Bruce Lee

At age 28, Valerie got her first job at a major hospital in the United States. She was a nurse. Even though she already had a master's degree, she recognized the advantage of adding an American education to her career. She enrolled at a U.S. college and got another master's degree. Despite the challenges associated with the stereotypes of her culture, being female, and being a single parent, she persisted and after many years, was appointed CEO of the hospital. Valerie served more than 10 years in that capacity.

Valerie's story is an example of one Caribbean American who migrated to the United States with the determination to succeed, and did. This chapter digs deeper with some background on who Caribbean Americans are, provides an historical perspective, and later provides details of their self-analysis of the path they took to achieve success.

Caribbean Americans are immigrants from the Caribbean islands who settled and attained citizenship in the United States. These countries include Antigua, and Barbuda, Aruba, the Bahamas, Barbados, Belize, the Cayman Islands, Cuba, Dominica, Haiti, Honduras, Grenada, Guyana, Jamaica, Montserrat, St. Kitts and Nevis, St. Lucia, St. Vincent and the Grenadines, Suriname, and Trinidad and Tobago. From a theoretical perspective, little is known about this population, which may be because the U.S. Census Bureau provides information in different ways to identify this group. Information revealed depends on the data source that is used.

Evolution in the United States

Against that background, it may be advantageous to include a historical perspective on the evolution of the path this ethnic group took to settle in the United States. Since Britain emancipated the Black slaves in its Caribbean colonies, West Indians have been on the move. Better opportunities lured many from regions of population surplus and underemployment, such as Barbados, to regions of population shortage and job opportunity, such as Trinidad. The most labor-intensive project was the French attempt to build a canal across

Panama with the help of West Indian immigrants. This failed at first, but subsequent to the United States gaining dominant power in the Caribbean, the canal was eventually built. Today, it connects the Pacific Ocean and the Caribbean Sea. West Indians were used in this project because of their willingness to work, their low labor costs, and lack of political interventions. This contributed to the first wave of immigrants.

The second wave of immigrants was related to those who arrived after the Johnson-Reed Act in 1924 and before the Hart-Cellar Act took effect in 1965. Many immigrants returned home during the Great Depression and World War II. However, after the postwar economic boom and when faced with the substandard economic living conditions in the Caribbean, they returned to the United States. In 1948, Britain passed the Nationality Act under which Commonwealth residents could enter at will. It was not surprising that by 1951, 17,000 West-Indian immigrant Blacks had taken advantage of this offer. This was short-lived, however, when the 1962 restrictions were implemented by the Parliament of the United Kingdom. Specifically, the Commonwealth Immigrants Act of 1962 made temporary provisions for controlling immigration into the United Kingdom. The third wave followed the Immigration and Nationality Act of 1965 that introduced hemisphere-wide quotas.

A variety of aspects assisted the formation and adaptation of Caribbean Americans in their new home. Like all other immigrants, Caribbean people in the

United States regularly compared their memories of home to the realities of their life in the new country. Caribbean people made efforts to retain their traditions of values and attitudes that create trust, justice, and social capital even under adverse conditions. They gained strength because they were socialized under relatively less oppressive environments. This led to greater self-confidence and self-worth despite the fact that in earlier decades, the ruling elites were Whites and light complexioned Creoles. On arrival in the United States, they approached the question of job search and willingness to work certain professions with attitudes different from their native Blacks. They were prepared to accept jobs that African Americans often shunned because of the low wages, low status, or generally poor working conditions. Hence, West Indian immigrants often reported negative impressions of native Black Americans; they looked down on this group for not being as enthusiastic about all the opportunities in the United States.

New York City became their preferred place of settlement and led to the integration of West Indian immigrants into the economy during the first 3 or 4 decades. Therefore, the New York City's Black community grew. Because they were not welcomed into White establishments, the Caribbean people acquired their own stores, shops, beauty parlors and barbershops, bars, real estate agencies, and restaurants. The skilled, white-collar, and semiprofessional occupations others had hoped to secure because of their middle-class status and education did not materialize. As a result, they had to settle for unskilled jobs even though these jobs were not commensurate with their education and skills. Many, therefore, opted for service-sector occupations. Unskilled workers were categorized as menial service workers, operatives, and manual laborers. They held jobs such as porters, waiters, or elevator operators. Later, they did jobs such as chauffeuring, occupations in the garment industry, and domestic work.

As the United States economy changed in the 1970s, 1980s, and 1990s, these Caribbean immigrants had to find new ways to make ends meet. This led to the manifestation of the ghetto communities where they were forced to live. The deregulation of the United States labor market in the late 1970s allowed the economic integration of illegal immigrants. This was the result of international efforts to reduce labor costs. A number of sweatshop jobs arose in response to the increasing importance of a secondary labor market (i.e., illegal workers hired by legitimate businesses). These included jobs such as security personnel, nursing aides, data-entry personnel, farm workers, babysitters, dog walkers, secretaries, messengers, machine operators, assemblers, and maids.

Caribbean American Heritage Month

Fast forward into the 21st century; Caribbean American leaders such as White House Champion of Change Dr. Claire Nelson, along with others, were advocates for recognition of this group. This eventually led to the establishment of the Caribbean American Heritage Month (CAHM). This initiative was established to fill the need to create and disseminate knowledge about the contributions of Caribbean immigrants to America. In addition, the organization was created to accomplish the goal of open dialogue between Caribbean people and the American public.

President Barack Obama, in his Presidential Proclamation to the 2012 CAHM, affirmed that Caribbean Americans have shaped every aspect of American society. This includes enhancing the arts and humanities as titans of music and literature, spurring the economy as intrepid entrepreneurs, making new discoveries as scientists and engineers, serving as staunch advocates for social and political change, and defending the ideals at home and abroad as leaders in the military.

Congresswoman Barbara Lee, in her keynote address for CAHM, emphasized that Americans of Caribbean ancestry reside in all areas of the United States. Throughout history, Caribbean Americans have served and contributed to the heritage of the United States through the arts, science, education, business, sports, military, and government.

Successful individuals of Caribbean American heritage include *Cicely Tyson*, Golden Globe Award-winning actress who was raised by her devoutly religious parents from the Caribbean island of Nevis; *Colin Powell*, the first African American appointed as the U.S. Secretary of State, and the first and so far the only to serve on the

Joint Chiefs of Staff, was the son of Jamaican immigrants. *Sir Sidney Poitier* was born while his Bahamian parents were on vacation in Miami, Florida. He became the first Black Academy Award winner for best actor in 1964, receiving the honor for his performance in "Lilies of the Field." *Jean Baptiste du Sable*, whose French father had migrated to Haiti and married his mother, is known as the first permanent resident of Chicago. *Claude McKay* was born in Jamaica and moved to Harlem in New York. He is known for his novels, essays, and poems including "If We Must Die." The Honorable *Shirley Chisholm* spent part of her childhood growing up with her grandmother in Barbados. She became the first African American Congresswoman.

Study Participants

The question remains: Were there common qualities that existed among those who achieved success in the United States? With the help of Nova Southeastern University and a phenomenological study, I decided to dig deeper.

Individuals in South Florida were identified who were successful at achieving the American Dream. Florida was selected because a majority of Caribbean immigrants (among others) initially settled in New York and then migrated to Florida. Migration southward was a way of maintaining connection with their home places where family, extended family, and friends lived.

The participants had an almost equal mixture of males and females. Participants who were interviewed had attained success through occupying a senior leadership position in an organization, a tenured academic position at a top-ranked United States university, a national honor, or a strong standing in the community in the United States. All participants were born in the Caribbean (Jamaica, Trinidad, Haiti, Nevis, and Cuba); except one who was born in the United Kingdom during the mass immigrant transit but was raised in the Caribbean. All became United States citizens or residents. Several were bilingual depending on their country of birth in the Caribbean.

Participants were leaders in community, business including real estate and radio or entertainment, healthcare, and academia, including teaching and leading research projects at top-ranked United States universities. Several had entrepreneurial capacities including founding their own companies and chambers of commerce; founding nonprofits, speaking in a variety of venues, and other charitable educational and community projects. A few others were involved in Unites States politics. Over 50% had received national awards in education, arts, business, healthcare, and philanthropy; others were involved in corporate America including a major television network, government agency, and aviation.

CHAPTER 5

THE UNVEILING: NARRATIVES OF THEIR JOURNEY

All you need in this life is ignorance and confidence, and then success is sure.

—Mark Twain

The selected Caribbean American leaders were asked what they believed were the characteristics that made them successful. Their self-exposed narratives were compiled under the top leadership traits.

Self-confidence. Self-confidence was a theme that all identified as a major characteristic of success. This theme is identified by the ability to be certain about one's competencies and skills. It includes a sense of self-esteem and self-assurance and the belief that one can make a difference and allows the leader to feel assured that his or her attempts to influence are appropriate and right.

Karen commented, "the desire to help people. To be a servant leader. To really help others to succeed. I think it's really the desire to help and to make a difference."

Gerline stated, "I think it's a strong sense of self and goals despite the stigma that's gonna be placed on you."

Maria commented, "Once you know what you want, you go get it. You work hard. No limits."

Nicole stated, "My personality and my interpersonal skills. I find it a joy because the challenge gives me a buzz. Is it always easy? No, but sometimes you make it look easy, and that's a gift."

Jacques expressed, "you want it? The road is available—go get it."

Derrick commented, "I believe when I got that leadership role, I was the right person for the job. I worked hard and I got the promotion because I was worth getting the promotion."

Donavan stated, "I think the first thing is just being ambitious and that comes from my heritage. Just the desire to succeed."

Richard remarked, "Believing in yourself. Believing that if you have a plan and if you move ahead with that plan through thick and thin, you will prevail. That's the biggest thing that helped me."

Self-discovery. Self-discovery refers to knowing one's individual strengths, talents, interests, and what one does well. It means having the ability to create a role that plays to one's particular strengths. Pertinent statements referring to this theme are as follows:

I was updating many of the residents on what was happening in the city far better than most of the elected officials . . . and then comments were made that you're actually the commissioner because you're . . .informing us as to what is going on than most of them that were there. (Moses)

Gerline commented, "And so I did a 6-year ethnography following a group of Haitian American kids and I feel that they sent me to school. They sent me to Harvard. They became my teachers."

Making the best of where I am, and stop resisting what is. And so, I find that's when things opened up for me. Things started looking better and then that allows you to see things in a different light . . . opportunities that are there sitting right in front of you and you're not even aware. (Donavan)

Horace commented, "it is the callers to our program who kept harping on me . . . why don't you run for elected office . . . then it kept coming . . . and it went on. And then I went to a few meetings and I'm saying hey, maybe. . . ."

I came to [Washington,] DC in the middle of the civil unrest in the country. I had to make adjustments and adjustments fast. So one of the first things I had to do was to adjust to the American way of living. Some of us in the group [university students] would try to hide within our cultures and others like me decided I'm gonna find out what this whole thing is about. So that has helped me, even now it helps me. (Richard)

Values/ethics. The traits of successful Caribbean Americans include strong values of honesty and integrity, and their foundation of leadership encompassed ethical leadership, principles of respect, service, justice, honesty, and a strong sense of community. Statements for this theme were as follows:

Moses pointed out, "I have been engaged in the broader community, so there are a lot of people from different areas that knew me and knew the work and knew my sincerity."

Karen commented, "if I'm put in a situation, my job is to make that better. Whatever I'm given, my job is to leave it in a better way than I found it. So that you can build it aggressively, and make things better and working and helping people."

Gerline shared, "people are disappointed that I'm not this cutthroat, back-stabbing individual."

Nicole commented, "meeting people where they are. Understanding people's abilities, socioeconomic situations."

Jacques stated, "constantly reminding myself of what is expected of me and what I expect of myself."

Derrick pointed out, "I believe my Christian life helped me to deal with a lot of these stress issues because I just felt that . . . if I'm here to do a job..."

Donavan commented, "to foresee the potential results of what your actions are gonna be."

Richard remarked, "because I still believe in integrity and morality."

Vision. All participants identified with vision as a major trait. This theme was identified by the ability to envision an uplifting and enabling future to have a dream, to have a mission, to see the pattern, and to establish goals for themselves.

I ran usually with a purpose in mind with definitive plans to accomplish certain things. It's not just about a contest to see how many people like me and showcase me. It was about trying to make a difference and doing something different. (Moses)

Karen commented, "know what you want in terms of your objectives, be very focused on those objectives . . . Be very focused and centered on those objectives . . . work hard . . . and you can achieve it."

You know I have a larger responsibility in this world than I could even imagine. For Haitian Americans, Caribbean

Americans, Blacks, White children globally . . . to understand who we are as the Caribbean American spirit. And also, I have a responsibility to my nation. I'm a global citizen that happens to be encased in a Haitian vessel, a Caribbean vessel. And as Caribbean people, we are Americans. The journey of the American story began in the Caribbean. We are African American. We are Caribbean Americans. We are global citizens of this world; and what do we have to contribute. (Gerline)

Maria stated, "I had it very clear that this was a mission and a transitional period. I had it clear from when I was 12 years old that this was a transitional period for me that…there were gonna be rough times."

Jacques commented, "when you and I as West Indians come here, we're not interested in looking for Black and White issues, we're looking for opportunities and success."

Donavan added, "we just try to accomplish what needs to be done."

Horace remarked, "one has to come to an understanding . . . you have a purpose."

Richard stated, "focusing on something and working hard on it and believing in it is what got me through, even when the chips were against me,"

Esmeralda commented, "it's always possible, and you know, it's never too late . . . never too late."

Humility was also a personal characteristic mentioned. Humility is defined here as what Jim Collins referred to as believing in good luck and possibilities beyond one's control, appreciating what life is giving, modest and willful, humility, and fearless. Pertinent statements regarding humility were as follows:

Karen communicated, "You have to be prepared to start over from the bottom. I came and I had a master's already, I was all of 28 years old, but I had to start from the very bottom."

Nicole commented, "I see myself . . . who I want to be. Positive, confident, down to earth." Horace observed, "I think it demands a certain . . . rejection of self and you know, but an acknowledgement."

Richard stated, "about 75% luck . . . and I think that was one of the most advantageous things that ever happened to me, and I think it happened purely by chance."

Commitment. This theme refers to the ability to establish challenges and expectations and apply oneself with focus and patience.

I said I was gonna enhance the way central . . . looked (56:50:50) . . . and get people involved and engaged in what was going on in the city and work toward solutions and building the economy of the city and helping the businesses grow. (Moses)

If you really work hard and you are really smart about how you're working and how you're building relationships, you will be successful. 'Cause after awhile people stop thinking of you as being somebody from Jamaica or the Caribbean. (Karen)

I decided that I was going to apply to one school. I was gonna go to Harvard to tell the stories of these Haitian American kids and how they transition into this country because no one else seemed to care. No one wanted to hear the story. They just wanted to label them. (Gerline)

Maria reflected, "I remember the guy goes 'this is a class of 30, and only 2 of you will work in the field.' And I remember thinking . . . I gotta be one of those. I gotta be one. I'm sorry, but I am one of those."

Jacques commented, "willingness and commitment. I am willing to sacrifice my own leisure and pleasures to commit to something that I know has meaning for the long run.

Donavan communicated, "I notice that you don't see yourself less than. You see yourself as anyone else. So you work hard at accomplishing whatever you need to accomplish. You don't see those barriers."

Persistence. Persistence as a theme describes several qualities including endurance and follow through as well as not giving up in pursuit of goals. All of the participants mentioned persistence as a personal trait that contributed to their success:

And it took me seven years to build this center for them. Professors don't get paid as much as people think, and I went to Haiti every summer. I went and worked with the young people and then during the summers I would do workshops with them. So I built it. (Gerline)

Jacques commented, "Wherever you wanna go . . . you probably can get there. It may not be easy, but you can get there." Derrick stated, "I think in any field, consistency always pays off, whether its sports or . . . any industry, you have to be consistent in your effort and not slack off."

Donavan expressed, "to do something, you have to do it until it's done." Richard commented, "the belief . . . that if you stick to it you'll succeed." Esmeralda communicated, "it's an immigrant mentality, in that we need to succeed no matter what. And we're going to do it—no matter what."

Optimistic. Optimism as a theme describes the outlook on challenges as the beginning of a new success and includes the willingness to tolerate frustration and delay with an optimistic outlook. Kouzes and Posner included searching out challenging opportunities to change, grow, innovate, and improve. All participants mentioned optimism as a personal trait.

You know success when you have pride and respect for yourself and the work that you're doing. We're human and we all make mistakes but if you are able to help another person understand and believe that they have the potential to create the impossible—I think that's success. (Gerline)

Maria commented, "it was a period of transitions and I was gonna go through it like anybody else would."

Donavan observed, "You don't see barriers. You don't have a negative attitude about yourself. You feel that you fit in . . . there is nothing there that will hold you back so you do what you do without envisioning a barrier."

Esmeralda communicated, "it's always possible and you know, it's never too late . . . never too late."

Family oriented. This theme is identified as respect for family values and familial influence including mother, father, and extended family. Participants mentioned that their family and family values had an impact on their personal traits. Relevant statements follow:

Gerline shared, "I think it's my grandmother. . . . She had this incredible life, and she persevered. She inspired me to have confidence in myself and use school as a tool to better my future."

Jacques communicated, "being something that my mom can be proud of. . . . I was driven to her, for her, and by her, and my responsibility was to ensure that I gave her a better life than she had, or the life that she inspired that I would have had."

Richard provided this statement:

Three simple principles. Daddy say first, let no one define for you what success is. You define what is success for you. Second thing, let no one define for you what is happiness. Third, my father believed strongly in integrity. Those kinds of principles are not very common—morality and integrity.

Drive. Drive is identified as having the desire to do more and more and to exercise initiative in social situations. All participants identified drive as a personal trait:

Gerline pointed out, "I became the thing that I didn't have. I started mentoring young people. So I felt that the way I could empower myself was to empower others. The way that I could contribute is to model my life as an example of success and perseverance."

That you can do it. You can do anything you want here. This is a great country. So many opportunities. I mean there's no excuse. If I came from nothing—I used to get up in the morning and I would touch soil, we didn't have cement in our house, and then to get up and touch carpet or tile is a blessing. (Maria)

Learner. The traits included in this category are the zeal for learning, education, teaching, sharing knowledge informally, learning from past experiences, pursuit of knowledge, and belief in lifelong learning. All of the participants mentioned being a learner as a personal trait.

Karen commented, "I don't take anything for granted, I never live on my laurels or try to talk about what I have achieved."

So education was not only academic education that you received mostly at school and there was also the education that you received at home. And that education at home was really having character, having self-confidence, having a sense of self, having a culture. (Gerline)

Donavan communicated, "My father just ringing in my ears, education is very important. That was always sitting in the back of my mind."

Horace stated, "any success I have had came from . . . making up my mind to go to school—tertiary institutions."

Richard pointed out, "me and my wife, both of us decided very early the most important thing is education."

Esmeralda commented, "Can you imagine knowing the language, going to school, being educated—what can you not do?"

Communication skills. The qualities included in this category are people skills, listening skills, public speaking skills, and articulation skills. All of the participants identified communication skills as an important trait.

Moses communicated, "being affable, being accessible, being open, and being transparent as much as you could be. But just getting out to know people and meet people. Being pleasant, being kind—not be angry." Nicole stated, "You have to be a good communicator. Listening—people want to be heard."

Passion. Being passionate was a theme that was identified by all of the participants as one of their major traits. They mentioned working hard and putting their heart into their jobs. Two relevant examples are provided:

Moses mentioned, "if you work hard enough, if you dedicate yourself; if you do what's right, you can overcome any obstacle and be pretty much anything that you want." Esmeralda commented, "Maybe I'm not going to be able to do this, but I'm going to try it, and I'll learn from it."

Responsibility. Taking responsibility for achieving what they think is important and the willingness to accept the consequences of their decisions and actions identify this theme. All participants mentioned responsibility as a major personal trait:

Karen expressed, "affirm to yourself that you're capable. . . . Find those people who are gonna be supportive, because they're out there." Maria communicated, "You have to have the discipline to do it. Willing to sacrifice time and family and all those things." Derrick stated, "I managed to perform on the highest level given the challenges."

Just accepting that the color of your skin once you're in this country is a determining factor in how you are sometimes treated. And so that was a shocker. I mean I didn't know that it would have so much of an impact on your life. But after you get over the initial shock, you're ok. Then you know how to deal with it. (Donavun)

Horace commented, "you don't give up on it. Find those things that make it work for you and do what you have to do."

CHAPTER 6

CHALLENGES ALONG THE WAY

You don't make progress by standing on the sidelines whimpering and complaining. You make progress by implementing ideas.

-Shirley Chisholm

The interview question was, "What challenges did you, as a Caribbean American leader, have to overcome?" This question was designed to identify challenges that these leaders have had to overcome in their lives. Four themes and patterns emerged.

Work-related challenges. The factors in this theme include lack of a professional network, job experience, and managing personalities. Of the participants, 95% encountered work-related challenges. Relevant statements on this theme were as follows:

I think the initial challenge that you have to overcome as brand new is that you really don't have any legacy, and you really don't have any contacts, and so the main challenge is to establish that professional networking linkage and build on it. (Karen)

Gerline explained, "People label you as a threat or they question, what are your motives? Like I have had people tell me, you graduated from Harvard; what's your academic game? You know I'm like, I don't got a game."

I think that it's unfortunate that in some fields Caribbean Americans face resistance from African Americans because some of us come here and do well and they believe it's at their expense. But I never believe I took a job from anyone. I believe when I got that leadership role, I was the right person for the job. I worked hard and I got the promotion because I was worth getting the promotion. (Derrick)

Cultural challenges. All participants experienced cultural challenges to overcome. The elements included in this theme were culture shock; individualist vs. collectivist culture; stereotyping; and discrimination based on national origin, gender, language, and accent.

Statements that pertained to this theme included Karen's comment, "when I was appointed CEO 10 years ago . . . you heard little whispers about she got the job because she was Black, she got the job because she was a woman, not because she was capable."

Gerline stated, "when I came to the U.S. at a very early age, I was put in remedial courses. And part of that had to do with not understanding how I expressed myself culturally."

Maria communicated, "I came as a child and I was light. So people would come and talk to me in English and I wouldn't know what they were talking about. So I wasn't identified as an American but I had the looks."

Nicole commented, "stereotype in terms of being a woman. Sometimes stereotype in terms of being Black and non-American. Total ignorance."

I had to subordinate my cultural beliefs or my cultural behaviors and subordinate my own native tongue. My accent had to be something that I had to abandon in order to communicate effectively and successfully with people. Rather than being looked at silly and . . . humorous, to some extent. (Jacques)

Donavan commented, "and just this typical stereotype. Mostly you might have an accent so people figure you don't know too much. And being a woman that you're not strong enough, you don't know enough and that type of thing."

Horace stated, "the biases that are directed at people who come from outside of the country. There have been times when language was a problem where people claim they don't understand you. Not true."

I think more because I'm a woman, the challenges were there. The gender was more like . . . what is a woman like you doing here? Because I was a woman moving into a very man—a male-dominated environment as is the legal field. (Esmeralda)

Social challenges. The facets of social challenges include the lack of social support, family-related challenges, and labeling. Participants cited social challenges.

Moses communicated, "…weren't born here. Sometimes being looked at as an outsider."

It was a period of adjustments, not only because I was migrating to another country and it was a different culture, and I was trying to find my way and who I wanted to be. And the age was difficult for anybody—it was a double whammy for me, becoming a teenager and the adult thing. So it was rather difficult. (Maria)

The first thing for me was the dynamics of the culture. You go through a culture shock when you come out of the Caribbean as a young kid, came into America, and then start a profession or life, because you were not socialized in that environment. One of the first shocks for me was the impersonality of life. People were not as cordial. (Jacques)

Financial challenges. The facets included in this theme are financial limitations or lack of money. Seventy percent of participants indicated financial constraints as a major challenge.

Gerline commented, "You know my mother couldn't pay the whole tuition and I was given that opportunity to have access to money." Maria communicated, "When we came here, my parents were so busy trying to survive themselves, and I tell my brother that we kind of made it on our own."

Derrick stated, "The first 2 years was rough because I felt that I made a mistake coming, and I couldn't find anything in my field."

"I saw about her school fees and my school fees before I paid my mortgage, before I paid my car note . . . all the way through the early years," Richard stated.

CHAPTER 7

NEW CULTURE: STEPS TO SUCCESS

Success is nothing more than a few simple disciplines, practiced every day.

-Jim Rohn

Study participants encountered the common challenges that were work related, cultural, social, and financial. But the question remained--how did they overcome the challenges? Essentially what strategies did they use? Five themes and patterns emerged from their individual responses pertaining to self-awareness, motivation, social skills, and the bicultural approach. These strategies are presented separately.

Self-awareness. Self-awareness was a theme for all participants. Attributes of this ability are self-confidence that shows itself by persuasiveness and realistic self-assessment and extends to a person's understanding of his or her strengths, values, and goals. The following are statements relating to this theme:

I constantly check myself. I study my weaknesses and my limitations and challenges and if I have the capacity, I make them better. If I don't, I get colleagues and family around me that can help with the limitation that I have. (Gerline)

Maria commented, "It was discipline. It was just knowing."

Faith, believing in yourself. Believing that if you have a plan and if you move ahead with that plan through thick and thin, you will prevail. That's the biggest thing that helped me get over it. Stay, stay on plan. (Richard)

Motivation. All participants identified motivation as a major theme. The components are having an optimistic outlook toward life, passion, and strong work ethic. The following statements are from interviews with participants:

Moses communicated, "being dedicated. Put the time and effort in when necessary to make things happen." Karen commented, "I think you have to ignore—block out the outside noise and understanding what is it that you want to achieve and go about it in a steadfast manner."

Social skills. Social skills were identified as a major theme by 90% of the participants. The components include building strong relationships, teamwork, community involvement, sharing, and communication skills. The following are excerpts from the transcripts:

Karen stated, "build alliances and build relationships, not only with your West Indian friends and associates, because at the end of the day, how you're perceived, is how you relate across the spectrum."

When you get to that place where you're established as somebody who can influence others, is to get to that place of being able to give back. I think life is about service - giving back. Giving back of your time, your finances (if you have it). It's not about wealth. It's about serving; it's about giving back; it's about being the best person I can be for the young people coming up because they're our future. They're our tomorrows and we have to invest in them; instill in them; make time for them. (Nicole)

Derrick remarked, "Mentoring was the most influential. Nothing I learnt in college really prepared me for leadership; it just gave me the stepping-stone."

Bicultural approach. Bicultural approach was a major theme among 80% of the participants. Bicultural approach refers to learning the work habits of both cultures, understanding the culture and the society, learning the system, becoming part of the society, and embracing both cultures. Statements that depict this theme were as follows:

The forces of Caribbean people in this country are very meaningful, especially in the Diaspora. But I think somehow we have not abandoned our own idiosyncrasies of individuality coming to America. And when you look out across the sea of people, and they're all Black from the Caribbean, you cannot identify who's from St. Kitts, Nevis, Trinidad, Barbados, unless they speak. So you now still become another West Indian. And I think it would help us greatly if we put a little bit more emphasis or a little bit more energy on harnessing the Caribbean strength of unity and power within the Diaspora to give a voice to Caribbean people that is much louder than it is at this point in time. (Jacques)

In cases where you have males or some not recognizing that you have the knowledge or the ability to do something, you just have to be strong and jut forceful. It just depends on who I was dealing with at the time; you adapt. You develop strategies of just accepting or resisting when necessary or not resisting when necessary. (Donavan)

Take the good things from our culture. Don't give up the culture from which you came. America is a very benevolent country. One thing this country has taught me, to be a benevolent human being. Care about the people around you. Give some. I take business and benevolence from this country. And all the rest seem to be the culture of the Caribbean—caring, integrity, church. (Richard)

Education. Factors included in education are attaining good, solid higher education, learning from success stories, and mentors. All participants had a good, solid education; 95% of them mentioned education as being a success strategy and 40% affirmed having mentors as their success strategy.

Education was not only academic education that you received mostly at school. There was education you received at home. And that education at home was really having character, having self-confidence, having a sense of self, having a culture. (Gerline)

When I finished high school and I didn't know what I wanted to be or do, I started reading. My mother would tell me to get an education. She was very firm on that. She was a teacher in Cuba and she was a believer in education. So I kinda knew that I had to do something. So I was aware and focused that that's what I had to do. (Maria)

CHAPTER 8

THE COMPARISON WITH OTHER ETHNIC GROUPS

Happiness lies in the joy of achievement and the thrill of creative effort.
-Franklin D. Roosevelt

Looking back, we spent some time researching the success strategies of Caribbean American Immigrant leaders. We considered the challenges they had to overcome and looked at how they overcame the challenges. Our findings revealed the various strategies used and these were explained before. But the desire was also to take it a step further to compare with another ethnic group to gain insights as to whether they experienced the same challenges, and used the same strategies to succeed. The ethnic group selected was Iranian American leaders because a similar study was conducted by Dr. Fereshteh Amin.

Iranian Americans Versus Caribbean Americans

Traits/characteristics. The results of the study verified that Iranian Americans and Caribbean Americans identified the same characteristics as being instrumental to their success, albeit in different variations. Both ethnic groups verified self-confidence, values, and vision as being instrumental. However, Caribbean Americans identified having persistence, optimism, drive, passion, responsibility, and learning at higher levels than did Iranian Americans. Conversely, self-discovery, humility, and creativity were higher among Iranian Americans when compared to Caribbean Americans.

Challenges. Results of the study verified that Iranian Americans and Caribbean Americans encountered challenges in the same areas of work related, culture, social, and financial. Both ethnic groups experienced financial challenges at similar levels. However, Iranian Americans encountered more work-related and social challenges than Caribbean Americans, whereas Caribbean Americans encountered more cultural challenges than did Iranian Americans.

Success strategies. The study also verified the results of success strategies that both ethnic groups used to overcome the challenges. These were identified as self-awareness, motivation, social skills, bicultural approach, and education. Both groups identified that high levels of self-awareness and motivation were instrumental to their success. However, Iranian Americans used skills that are more social (e.g. building strong relationships, teamwork, community involvement, sharing, and communication skills); along with the bicultural approach (i.e. learning the work habits of both cultures, understanding the culture and the society, learning the system, becoming part of the society, and embracing both cultures) to overcome the challenges. On the other hand, the use of education was higher among Caribbean Americans.

Influential factors. The study also verified the results that the most influence on the success of both Iranian Americans and Caribbean Americans fell among the themes of traits, events, and family. The level of personal traits and events was higher among Iranian Americans, whereas family was higher among Caribbean Americans as being more influential to the two ethnic groups' success.

Naturally, it is difficult to generalize across the entire population of Caribbean-Americans based on this study alone. However, the results are synonymous with *Amin's* studies on success strategies of Iranian-Americans as well as with *Gladwell's* study on success, which emphasized that success is a function of persistence, doggedness, and the willingness to work hard. It is synonymous with *Berg's* encouragement to anticipate (as in vision), and create everything twice—first in individuals' minds and then in physical reality. It is also synonymous with *Mendoza's* study on Latino business owners that identified nine themes that included family, being visible in the local community, tenacity and perseverance, optimism, and personal sacrifices among others.

Finally, it is synonymous with Jim Collins study regarding the qualities of good-to-great leaders that included self-effacing, quiet, reserved, or shy, and leaders who showed a paradoxical blend of personal humility and professional will.

Equally important, the results of this study are also consistent with leadership theories that leadership varies according to culture, trait, ability, skill, and approach. The approach selected depends on the circumstances and situation.

Furthermore, the results of the interviews with Caribbean-Americans affirmed the argument that leadership is not easy but those who dare to lead can have a major impact on themselves, business situations and the people they lead. The participants in this study were chosen because each leader had attained success through occupying a senior leadership position in an organization, a tenured academic position at a top ranked United States university, a national honor, or a strong standing in the community in the United States within the years 2006-2013. Therefore, the result of this study illustrated the impact that selected leaders have had on themselves, those they lead, and their community.

CHAPTER 9

NOW IT'S YOUR TURN

The difference between a successful person and others is not a lack of strength, not a lack of knowledge, but rather a lack of will.

-Vince Lombardi

In a chain of events that led to the restructuring of one organization, I was present when one Caribbean American immigrant was being terminated because of changes in the company. I must confess that I have done more restructuring in organizations than meets the eye. We live in a time of change. The middle aged woman bawled and wailed lamenting the words "don't send me home! It's my life! It's my life!" Despite numerous comforts that we would assist her with finding another job, she was relentlessly reluctant. The problem? She came from the Caribbean where she believed commitment to one organization was, as she put it, "her life." When it was being pulled away, she did not know what to do.

Do you know why some people succeed while others don't? It's simple. I'll use the story of renowned author Stephen King.

Stephen King began his writing career encountering numerous rejections. A man of limited means at the time, he wrote many books, sent them to publishers, and was rejected. What stands out most is that as he received these rejections, he decided to post the letters on his wall as a reminder.

As time went by, he wrote one story that he did not feel connected to. Discouraged, he threw it in the trash. Sometime later, his wife saw the manuscript in the trash and for some reason, she pulled it out, read it, and was hooked. When King got home, she told him how good it was and that he should complete it. He did and subsequently sent the book *Carrie* to publishers, who paid him an advance of $2,500! Elated, he spent the advance on a few much-needed items and continued his meagre teaching career. Months later, he was told that Signet Books had bought the paperback rights and he would receive $200,000! Imagine his joy! Today, Stephen King is a household name through his petrifying books and daunting movies!

So, does the story of Stephen King encourage you to press on and never give up? King was a normal, everyday person like you and me. But what he did differently was to keep at it. He had the never-give-up attitude. He surrounded himself with good supporters like his wife, who was there to support him when the going got tough.

That's the reason some people are successful while others aren't. They never give up. Successful people press on even when they become discouraged. They have mentors, close friends, and confidantes who they turn to when the going gets tough. Remember that success means different things to different people. To be successful, you have got to stick to it. Never give up on your dreams! Your goals! Your aspirations!

In a short while, you will be able to use the soon-to-be-published workbook *Success Strategies* as a guide to help steer your dreams to reality…to your success.

Johann Wolfgang Von Goethe reminded us that "what is not started will never get finished." This simple quote differentiates those who are successful from those who choose to sit by and wait for things to happen. Successful people such as the Caribbean Americans espoused in this phenomenological study never "sit on their laurels" and wait for things to happen. They act.

When the study began back in 2010, research revealed that the United States Census Bureau projected a growth in the population from over 282 million in 2000 to almost 336 million in 2020. However, in March 2015, the Census Bureau revised the projection that the United States is expected to become a majority-minority nation in 2044 for the first time (Colby & Ortman, 2015). As a consequence, this research will provide immigrants and struggling groups with the inspiration to have hope and adopt the attitude that they, too, can become successful and achieve their dream.

So get started today. I have summarized the strategies to assist you to get the ball rolling. Follow these success tips and pull on the knowledge of why some people succeed and others don't.

1. Enhance your Dream. Find your passion and make it Big!
2. Strategize your Success through Berg's personal strategies:
    a. Aim through creating your own personal definition of success;
    b. To achieve goals you must Anticipate as in creating everything twice; first in your minds and then in physical reality
    c. Through Audacity, you should get rid of negative attitudes and fear-of-failure or disapproval which is a critical barrier to success
    d. Focus on Action which helps you overcome destructive habits such as indecisiveness, procrastination, and over-planning.
    e. Act as though you have succeeded through affiliating with successful people, maintaining learning, mental and physical fitness and rewarding small success.
    f. Learn to Adapt. Be flexible. Think outside the box. Risk the pain of possible failure and pursue new achievements.

3. Embrace the five strategies of success uncovered in this study:
   a. Self-Awareness: Self-confidence; self-discovery; vision
   b. Motivation: Drive, passion, work ethic; optimistic outlook
   c. Social Skills: Build strong relationships; get involved with your community
   d. Bi-cultural approach: Embrace cultures of different groups, not just your own
   e. Education: Be a learner
4. Develop the dedication and determination to succeed no matter the odds.
5. Do the right thing.
6. Get along with others.
7. Keep the Passion alive. As Steve Jobs said to Stanford graduates, "Stay Hungry."

That said, if you want to be successful, you must follow your heart. Follow your passion. To lead yourself, you must believe in your ability. If you strongly believe something in your ability—Go for it! Reach for the stars! As Mahatma Gandhi said, *"Be the change you wish to see in the world"*. More than likely, you will achieve with dedication and hard work.

EPILOGUE

Be the Change You Wish to See in the World.
                                                    -Mahatma Gandhi

The youth referred to at the start of this book was my brother Devon. He slipped into a state of apathy and hopelessness, a state from which he never returned—dying tragically before my final intervention.

I now use this experience as the drive to fuel my passion to see youths and adults in transition accomplish their dreams. The intention is that with defined goals and aspirations, they, too, can achieve success.

Delving a little more into my background, I left high school, had my first child Monique, and then got my first job as a receptionist/secretary. I didn't have a dream. From humble beginnings, I just thought you get a job after high school and that was it. Then a colleague at work asked me if I wasn't going back to school. It felt like a strange question.

I left that job to work with a large commercial bank where I started my studies. A year later, I received the Certified Professional Secretary designation—passing the required six subjects all at once—and received recognition. Fast forward to 6 years later: I landed into my career with a major international pharmaceutical company to manage their Human Resource portfolio. I had responsibility for the Northern Caribbean countries reporting into the Latin American region for over 14 years. Rising from someone who didn't have a goal to achieve an education I gained Bachelors in Business Management, Master of Science in Human Resource Management, Master's in Healthcare Administration, and Doctor of Education with a major in Organizational Leadership.

This book is now my driving force to connect youths to *Dream* and then create a plan to accomplish that dream. The workbook on Success Strategies provides more details on how to create that plan. Dare I say, if you don't know where you're going, you will end up some place else. To youths at large and my daughters Monique and Ashleigh, I challenge you to create a plan and start your journey to success today.

DEFINITION OF TERMS

Success. This term refers to the attainment of wealth, position, and honors (Amin, 2006). The concept of success was espoused as getting what a person wants with rewards that are sustainable for individuals and those for whom they care. Amin revealed four components based on her research about high achievers: happiness, achievement, significance, and legacy. Amin also claimed that success that encompasses all four accomplishments is more enriching and lasting.

Leader. This refers to a person who influences a group of individuals in the process of achieving a common goal. On the other hand, leadership is a *process* whereby a person influences a group of individuals to achieve a common goal (Northouse, 2001). Kouzes and Posner (2007) restated the Gilstrap statement that leadership is in the eyes of other people. The authors further shared the facets of leadership practices that emerged from thousands of personal-best cases. They highlighted five tenets of leadership: model the way, inspire a shared vision, challenge the process, enable others to act, and encourage the heart.

Leadership development. This term refers to an individual's self-development. Kouzes and Posner (2007) articulated that engineers have computers; painters, canvas and brushes; musicians, instruments; but leaders have only themselves. The instrument of leadership is the self, and mastery of the art of leadership comes from mastery of the self. Self-development is not about acquiring a lot of new information or trying out the latest technique. It is about leading out of what is already in one's soul. It is about liberating the leader within oneself. It is about setting oneself free (Kouzes & Posner, 2007).

Strategic leadership. This phrase refers to a person's ability to anticipate, envision, maintain flexibility, think strategically, and work with others to initiate changes that will create a viable future for the organization (Hopen, 2010).

Phenomenological study. This term describes the meaning of several individuals of their lived experiences of a concept or phenomenon. Phenomenologists focus on describing what all participants have in common as they experience a phenomenon (Creswell, 2007).

Diaspora. This refers to the movement of specific people to several societies together with the communities that they constructed (Palmer, 2000).

Nativity status. The U.S. Census Bureau (2011) defined this term as referring to whether a person is native or foreign born. The nativity status refers to anyone who was a U.S. citizen at birth. Individuals who were born in the United States, Puerto Rico, a U.S. island area such as U.S. Virgin Islands, Guam, American Samoa, the Commonwealth of the Northern Mariana Islands, or abroad of a U.S. citizen parent or parents, are defined as ***native born.*** The foreign-born population includes anyone who was not a U.S. citizen at birth, including those who have become U.S. citizens through naturalization.

Caribbean Americans and West Indian Americans. These two terms are used interchangeably. Caribbean Americans are immigrants from the English-speaking Caribbean islands who settled and attained citizenship in the United States. These countries include Antigua and Barbuda, the Bahamas, Barbados, Belize, the Cayman Islands, Dominica, Grenada, Guyana, Jamaica, Montserrat, St. Lucia, St. Vincent and the Grenadines, Suriname, and Trinidad and Tobago (Henke, 2001). In addition, non-English-speaking countries of Cuba and Haiti will be included in the study because of their location.

REFERENCES

Acosta, Y. D., & De La Cruz, G. P. (2011). The foreign born from Latin America and the Caribbean: 2010. Retrieved from
http://www.census.gov/prod/2011pubs/acsbr10-15.pdf

Ahmadian, A., & Amin, F. (2008). Successful strategies of foreign-born American leaders. Journal of American Academy of Business, 13(2), 45-51. Retrieved from ProQuest database. (Document ID No. 222869704)

Alliance for Excellent Education. (2006). Demography as destiny: Alliance finds that low minority graduation rates and rising minority populations could jeopardize the nation's economic future. Retrieved from
http://www.all4ed.org/publication_material/straight_as/6/20/#1

Amerindian. (2006). In E. Wright (Ed.), A dictionary of world history.
doi:10.1093/acref/9780192807007.001.0001/acref-9780192807007-e-129

Amin, F. (2006). Success strategies of Iranian American leaders. (Doctoral dissertation). Retrieved from ProQuest Dissertations and Theses database. (Document ID No. 304908351)

Beine, M., Docquier, F., & Özden, Ç. (2011). Diasporas. Journal of Development Economics, 95(1), 30-41.

Retrieved from ProQuest database. (Document ID No. 854033289)

Benzing, C., Chu, H. M., & Kara, O. (2009). Entrepreneurs in Turkey: A factor analysis of motivations, success factors, and problems. Journal of Small Business Management, 47(1), 58-91. Retrieved from ProQuest database. (Document ID No. 220959900)

Berg, D. H. (1996). Keys to self-designed success. The Journal for Quality and Participation, 19(2), 80-83. Retrieved from ProQuest database. (Document ID No. 219175732)

Brettell, C. B. (2011). Experiencing everyday discrimination: A comparison across five immigrant populations. Race and Social Problems, 3, 266-279. doi:10.1007/s12552-011-9055-1

Buchholz, T. G. (2007). New ideas from dead CEOs: Lasting lessons from the corner office. New York, NY: Harper Collins.

Clark, W. A. (2003). Immigrants and the American dream: Remaking the middle class. New York, NY: Guilford.

Clawson, J. G. (2009). Level three leadership: Getting below the surface (4th ed.). Upper Saddle River, NJ: Pearson Prentice Hall.

Collins, J. (2001). Good to great: Why some companies make the leap . . . and others don't. New York, NY: Harper Business.

Creswell, J. W. (2007). Qualitative inquiry and research design: Choosing among five approaches. Thousand Oaks, CA: Sage.

Creswell, J. W. (2008). Educational research: Planning, conducting, and evaluating quantitative and qualitative research. (3rd ed.). Upper Saddle River, NJ: Pearson Education.

Cullen, J. (2003). The American Dream: A short history of an idea that shaped a nation. New York, NY: Oxford University Press.

Dennis, J. (2005, September). A success worth having. Profit, 24(4), 21. Retrieved from ProQuest database. (Document ID No. 219223314)

Diaz, J. (2011). Immigration policy, criminalization, and the growth of the immigration industrial complex: Restriction, expulsion and eradication of undocumented in the U.S. Western Criminology Review, 12(2), 35-54. Retrieved from
http://wcr.sonoma.edu/v12n2/Diaz.pdf

Duncan, A. (2012). TIME Magazine names Jeremy Lin '10 one of the world's 100 most influential people. TIME Magazine. Retrieved from
http://www.time.com/time/specials/packages/article/0,28804,2111975_2111976,00.html

Eubanks, D. L., Antes, A. L., Friedrich, T. L., Caughron, J. J., Blackwell, L. V., . . . Mumford, M. D. (2010). Criticism and outstanding leadership: An evaluation of leader reactions and critical outcomes. Leadership Quarterly, 21, 365-368. Retrieved from ProQuest database. (Document ID No. 521178016)

Fallon, J. E. (2002). The American dream: Can it survive the 21st century? The Journal of Social, Political, and Economic Studies, 27, 386-392. Retrieved from ProQuest database. (Document ID No. 216800189)

Filisko, G. M. (2012). Chasing the dream. ABA Journal, 98(5), 46-53. Retrieved from ProQuest database. (Document ID No. 1015032842)

Foner, N. (2005). In a new land: A comparative view of immigration. New York: New York University Press.

Forck, M. (2010). Lessons from a legend. Professional Safety, 55(9), 20-21. Retrieved from ProQuest database. (Document ID No. 755054180)

Fry, L. W. (2003). Toward a theory of spiritual leadership. Leadership Quarterly, 14, 693-727. Retrieved from ProQuest database. (Document ID No. 200772219)

Gibbs, N., & Duffy, M. (2012, April 23). Inside the Presidents Club. TIME Magazine. Retrieved from http://www.time.com/time/magazine/article/0,9171,2111791,00.html

Gilkes, A. D. (2007). The West Indian Diaspora: Experiences in the United States and Canada. New York, NY: LFB Scholarly.

Gladwell, M. (2008). Outliers, the story of success. New York, NY: Little, Brown.

Glesne, C. (2006). Becoming qualitative researchers: An introduction. Boston, MA: Pearson Education.

Goleman, D. (2001). Harvard Business Review on what makes a leader. Boston MA: Harvard Business School Press.

Goleman, D., Boyatzis, R., McKee, A. (2004). Primal leadership: Learning to lead with emotional intelligence. Boston MA: Harvard Business School Press.

Greenbaum, S. D. (2002). More than Black: Afro-Cubans in Tampa. Gainesville: University of Florida Press.

Greer, M. E. (2011). Dare to lead. Professional Safety, 56(6), 30-31. Retrieved from ProQuest database. (Document ID No. 883866307)

Grieco, E. M. (2009). Race and Hispanic origin of the foreign-born population in the United States, 2007: American community survey reports. Washington, DC: U.S. Census Bureau.

Heffernan, M. (2010, March). Driven to succeed. Reader's Digest, 176, 63. Retrieved from ProQuest database. (Document ID No. 222495017)

Henke, H. (2001). The West Indian Americans. Westport, CT: Greenwood.

Hernandez, I., Mendoza, F., Lio, M., Latthi, J., & Eusebio, C. (2011). Things I'll never say: Stories of growing up undocumented in the United States. Harvard Educational Review, 81, 500-507. Retrieved from ProQuest database. (Document ID No. 896133404)

Hernandez-Reguant, A. (2005). Cuba's alternative geographies. The Journal of Latin American and Caribbean Anthropology, 10, 275-313.

Hopen, D. (2010). The changing role and practices of successful leaders. The Journal for Quality and Participation, 33(1), 4-9. Retrieved from ProQuest database. (Document ID No. 219117101)

Iyer, R. D. (2012). Servant or leader?: Who will stand up please? International Journal of Business and Social Science, 3(9). Retrieved from ProQuest database. (Document ID No. 010396374)

Jackson, S., Farndale, E., & Kakabadse, A. (2003). Executive development: Meeting the needs of top teams and boards. The Journal of Management Development, 22, 185-265. Retrieved from ProQuest database. (Document ID No. 216294697)

Johnson, C. (2006). Health as culture and nationalism in Cuba. Canadian Journal of Latin American & Caribbean Studies, 31(61), 91-113. Retrieved from ProQuest database. (Document ID No. 220236650)

Jones, T. (2009). Migration theory in the domestic context: North-South labor movement in Brazil. Human Architecture, 7(4), 5-14. Retrieved from ProQuest Social Science Journals database. (Document ID No. 1884329681)

Kara, O., Chu, H. M., & Benzing, C. (2010). Determinants of entrepreneur's success in a developing country. Journal of Business and Entrepreneurship, 22(2), 1-15. Retrieved from ProQuest database. (Document ID No. 762999334)

Knight, F. W. (2011). Cuba. In The Oxford Companion to the Politics of the World (2nd ed.). Retrieved from http://www.oxfordreference.com/views/html?subview=Main&entry=t121.e0170

Kouzes, J. M., & Posner, B. Z. (2007). The leadership challenge (4th ed.). San Francisco, CA: John Wiley & Sons.

Kugel, C., & Zuroweste, E. L. (2010). The state of health care services for mobile poor populations: History, current status, and future challenges. Journal of Health Care for the Poor and Underserved, 21, 422-429. Retrieved from ProQuest database. (Document ID No. 220585934)

Lee, B. (2012). National Caribbean American Heritage Month. Retrieved from http:// caribbeanamericanmonth.org/home

Locke L. F., Silverman S. J., & Spirduso, W. W. (2010). Reading and understanding research. Thousand Oaks, CA: Sage.

Meacham, J. (2012, July 2). Making of America: Keeping the dream alive. Time Magazine. Retrieved from http://www.time.com/time/specials/packages/article/0,28804,2117662_2117682_2117680,00.html#ixzz2Twbdu4Re

Mendoza, C. M. (2007). Hispanic entrepreneurs overcoming the odds of failure: A phenomenological study of Latino business owners (Doctoral dissertation). Retrieved from ProQuest Dissertations & Theses database. (Document ID No. 304733410)

Milk, L. (2009). Secrets of success. Washingtonian, 46(2), 44. Retrieved from ProQuest database. (Document ID No. 217619424)

Minderhout, D. J. (2006). More than Black: Afro-Cubans in Tampa. American Anthropologist, 108, 592-593. doi:10.1525/aa.2006.108.3.592

Model, S. (2008). West Indian immigrants: A Black success story? New York, NY: Russell Sage Foundation.

Murari, K. (2011). Just! five distinct leadership styles. International Journal of Research in Commerce and Management, 2(12), 30-36. Retrieved from ProQuest database. (Document ID No. 963632801)

Norris, T. S. (2011). Grow your leadership skills. Professional Safety, 56(8), 1-1. Retrieved from ProQuest database. (Document ID No. 904987990)

Northouse, P. G. (2001). Leadership: Theory and practice. Thousand Oaks, CA: Sage.

Northouse, P. G. (2007). Leadership: Theory and practice (4th ed.). Thousand Oaks, CA: Sage.

Obama, B. (2012). Presidential proclamation—National Caribbean-American Heritage Month, 2012. Retrieved from http://www.whitehouse.gov/the-press-office/2012/06/01/presidential-proclamation-national-caribbean-american-heritage-month-201

Oceania. (2010). In Oxford Dictionary of English. Retrieved from http://www .oxfordreference .com/search?siteToSearch=aup&q=Oceania&searchBtn =Search&isQuickSearch=true

Owen, C., Javalgi, R., & Scherer, R. (2007). Success strategies for expatriate women managers in China. Review of Business, 27(3), 24-31. Retrieved from ProQuest database. (Document ID No. 220959549)

Packer, G. (2012). The broken contract: Inequality and American decline. Current, 90(6), 20-31. Retrieved from Retrieved from ProQuest database. (Document ID No. 1023034514)

Palmer, C. A. (2000). Defining and studying the modern African Diaspora. The Journal of African-American History, 85(1), 27-32.

Pinnington, A. H. (2011). Leadership development: Applying the same leadership theories and development practices to different contexts? Leadership (London), 7, 335-365. doi:10.1177/ 1742715011407388

Punnett, B. J., Nurse, L., Duffy, J. A., Fox, S., Gregory, A., Lituchy, T., . . . Santos, N. M. B. F. (2007). Professionally successful women: Some evidence from the English-speaking Caribbean. Canadian Journal of Latin American & Caribbean Studies, 32, 121-154, 249-251. Retrieved from ProQuest database. (Document ID No. 220252950)

Rule, N. O., & Ambady, N. (2009). She's got the look: Inferences from female chief executive officers' faces predict their success. Sex Roles, 61, 644-652. doi:10.1007/s11199-009-9658-9

Schieman, S., Yuko, K. W., & Van Gundy, K. (2006). The nature of work and the stress of higher status. Journal of Health and Social Behavior, 47, 242-57. Retrieved from ProQuest database. (Document ID No. 201662170)

Shambaugh, R. (2010). The secrets of resilient leaders. Leader to Leader, 2010(58), 39-44. doi:10 .1002/ltl.440

Shaw-Taylor, Y., & Tuch, S. A. (Eds.). (2007). The other African-Americans: Contemporary African and

Caribbean immigrants in the United States. Lanham, MD: Rowan & Littlefield.

Smith, J. A., Flowers, A., & Larkin, M. (2012). Interpretative phenomenological analysis. Thousand Oaks, CA. Sage.

Strmic-Pawl, H., & Leffler, P. K. (2011). Black families and fostering of leadership. Ethnicities, 11(2), 139-162. doi:10.1177/ 1468796811398825

Sztompka, P. (2005). Editorial: Europe strikes back. European Review, 13, 165-168. Retrieved from ProQuest database. (Document ID No. 217344288)

Taleghani, G., Salmani, D., & Taatian, A. (2010). Survey of leadership styles in different cultures. Iranian Journal of Management Studies, 3, 91-111.

Thornton, S., & Curtis, J. W. (2012). A very slow recovery: The annual report on the economic status of the profession, 2011-12. Academe, 98(2), 4-15. Retrieved from ProQuest database. (Document ID No. 1010359863)

Uwaoma, U., & Reed, H. L. (2013). The challenges of increasing racial diversity in health care. Physician Executive, 39(1), 64-70. Retrieved from ProQuest database. (Document ID No. 1284082993)

Vogt, W. P. (2007). Quantitative research methods for professionals. Boston, MA: Pearson Education.

Warner, J. (2012, March 12). High-status stress. TIME Magazine. Retrieved from http://www.time.com/time/magazine/article/0,9171,2108019,00 .html

Waters, M. C., & Reed, U. (2007). The new Americans: A guide to immigration since 1965. Cambridge, MA: Harvard University Press.

ABOUT THE AUTHOR

Dr. Shelly Cameron is founder and managing Principal of Cameron Calder & Associates. She was born in Kingston, Jamaica and now lives in the United States. A Transition Coach, she specializes in helping busy management professionals take the steps to get out of their comfort zone to do the things they have always wanted to do.

Dr. Cameron is especially skilled in the healthcare industry, where she has worked for over 20 years, including 14 years as Head of Human Resources for countries in the Northern Caribbean, with leadership in the Latin America region for the International Pharmaceutical giant, GlaxoSmithKline. She directed Leadership and Change Management initiatives during several international mergers, which culminated into the coveted Employer of Choice Award. She also managed strategic initiatives of medical clinics across South Florida.

Dr. Cameron holds Doctorate in Education, major in Organizational Leadership, Masters in Healthcare Administration, Master of Science in Human Resource Management, and Bachelors in Management Studies.

On an individual basis, Dr. Cameron's mission is to inspire others to discover who they are and to become their best possible self, both professionally and in their life long career endeavors. At the community level through participation in workshops, health fairs and more, Dr. Cameron has collaborated with several organizations to contribute to the needy throughout the USA, Caribbean, and Kenya, East Africa. Her mission is to not only make a difference in the local community, but also to the wider society.

Through this book on Success Strategies of Immigrant American Leaders, Dr. Cameron reveals the results of a phenomenological study conducted with Nova Southeastern University that explored the hidden secrets of successful Immigrant American Leaders. She now connects it to those aspiring to achieve. Individuals are challenged to take that first step to accomplish their dreams, their goals, and their aspirations. As Author, Speaker, Transition Coach and Human Resource Consultant, Dr. Cameron devotes her life to connect others to success.

For Speaking and coaching needs, contact scameron@ccahr.com, or www.shellycameron.com.

ADDITIONAL OFFERINGS FROM THE AUTHOR

Services Include:

- Keynote Speeches
- Leadership and Success Coaching (one-on-one and in small groups)
- Consulting
- Seminars/Workshops
- Online blogs (sign up at www.successfulleaders.net)
- Brand You Seminars

Most Requested Keynote Speeches

- Managing Your People: Managing Your Business
- Your Career: Steps to Success
- Smart Hiring Techniques for Small Business Owners
- Leading Leaders
- Women in Business: Rising Success

Dr. Shelly Cameron is author of book on Success Strategies. In it she describes Why Some Individuals Succeed While Others Don't. Please hire her to Speak, Ask a Question or follow her Blog.

Twitter/https://twitter.com/DrShellyC

Instagram/https://www.instagram.com/drshellyc_success/

Facebook/https://www.facebook.com/DrShellyCameron/?fref=ts

WORK WITH ME

Here are ways to learn from my knowledge and experience

1. Search my Blog/https://successfulleaders.net/

Find inspirations for success

2. Subscribe to my updates

I write on Inspirations for Personal/Professional Development, Success, and more

3. Buy my Book.

Read my Research titled **The Leadership Challenge** in The Journal of American Academy of Business Cambridge (JAABC), 3/2016.

Get a copy of my book titled Success Strategies Workbook, available on Amazon.com. I have other products coming soon including inspirations titled GreenLight.

4. Book me as a Speaker.

I have been speaking publicly for over 10 years. I have given keynote, spoken at Events for Corporations, Nonprofits, Chambers of Commerce,

Clubs, Community events, and Churches. If you would like me to speak at your next event, please email me at scameron@ccahr.com.

5. **Hire me as your personal transition coach.**

I help busy management professionals get out of their comfort zone to do the things they have always wanted to do.

If you would like anything else, don't hesitate! Just contact me!

www.successfulleaders.net

shellycameron.com

BOOKS AND PUBLICATIONS

Research Publication, Journal of American Academy of Business (JAABC)

The Leadership Challenge at www.jaabc.com.

Success Strategies Workbook

Want to Succeed? Here's How

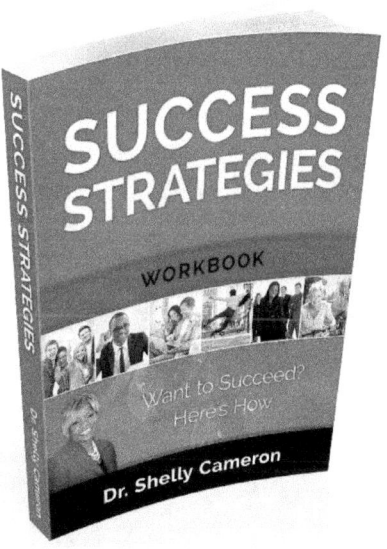

www.ingramcontent.com/pod-product-compliance
Lightning Source LLC
LaVergne TN
LVHW051846080426
835512LV00018B/3094